Original title:
Frost's Gentle Hand

Copyright © 2024 Creative Arts Management OÜ
All rights reserved.

Author: Cameron Blair
ISBN HARDBACK: 978-9916-94-512-4
ISBN PAPERBACK: 978-9916-94-513-1

Beneath the Glacial Canopy

Beneath the trees, the chill is brisk,
Squirrels in sweaters, oh what a risk!
Snowflakes giggle as they descend,
Each twist and turn, a jolly friend.

Icicles dangle like teeth so white,
A penguin slips, what a silly sight!
Snowmen gossip with frosty breath,
They joke of winter's pretzel death.

The Delicate Dance of Frosted Leaves

Leaves prance about with a shiver and shake,
Making a fuss as they wiggle and quake.
Branches chuckle, 'Oh, what a scene!'
While squirrels play tag, feeling quite keen.

Pinecones tumble, a clumsy affair,
Landing on noses, quite beyond compare!
The ground is a stage, for an icy ballet,
As nature performs in a chuckle-filled way.

Memories Caught in the Cold Light

Once there was snow, that danced in the night,
  Snowmen with hats, what a comical sight!
  A carrot for a nose, with a wink and a grin,
  He mocks the sun, 'You're not getting in!'

  Chilly memories, frozen mid-laugh,
  A snow angel flops, on a frozen giraffe.
  Caught in the light, all glimmering white,
  Whispers of winter, in laughter, take flight.

Evensong from a Winter's Heart

As evening falls, the sky turns blue,
A chorus of crickets where cold's diced and skewed.
A bear in pajamas, slipping about,
Trying to dance to the frosty clout.

Snowflakes pirouette, in a soft, quiet hum,
While rabbits play hopscotch, 'Hey, here I come!'
Laughter rings out, bright as the moon,
As winter sings softly, a frosty cartoon.

Shimmering Veils of Winter Light

Sparkling crystals dance and twirl,
Each one giggles, quite a whirl.
Snowflakes tickle noses bright,
While snowmen wear scarves loaded tight.

Icicles hang like daggers bold,
But dressed in sun, they're purest gold.
Children laugh, they leap and slide,
As fluffy flakes join in the ride.

Quietude at the Edge of Winter

In silent streets, the snowflakes play,
They tiptoe softly, come what may.
A squirrel in boots, looks quite a sight,
Chasing shadows, what a delight!

The trees are draped in blankets white,
While bushes shiver, they quiver tight.
Laughter echoes in the chill,
As hot cocoa warms, oh what a thrill!

Harmonies in the Winter's Breath

The wind hums tunes, a merry song,
Bouncing off rooftops all day long.
A penguin waddles, slips, then falls,
While giggles resonate through the halls.

Chill in the air, it gives us pause,
As nature chuckles, just because.
With frosty breath, we puff and grin,
What a winter, let the fun begin!

Silvery Flickers of a Frozen Dream

Under the moon, the snowflakes gleam,
Creating visions, a sparkly dream.
A rabbit hops, does a silly jig,
While deer prance forth, so small and big.

Snowball fights make laughter bloom,
As fluffy clouds drift, they loom.
With every flurry that lightly lands,
Winter giggles, full of plans.

The Caress of Winter's Glow

Snowflakes dance with quite the flair,
Giving hats to folks unaware.
The chill bites at a nose or two,
As laughter echoes through the blue.

Icicles hang like a silly grin,
As winter's chill sneaks in to win.
Snowmen chuckle, round and bright,
Waving hello in pure delight.

A Mosaic of Glacial Dreams

In the park, a slide of ice,
Kids zoom down, oh, that's precise!
But parents gather, 'til the last
To slip and slide, what a contrast!

Cocoa spills on wooly coats,
While penguin waddles steal the votes.
Each frosty breath, a puffy cloud,
As laughter bursts, oh so loud!

Threads of Ice in the Evening Light

Evening arrives with glimmer and gleam,
Stars twinkle down, a shining beam.
But who needs stars when laughter reigns,
As mittens hop on snowmen's brains?

A snowball flies, oh what a throw!
Direct hit, a face full of snow!
Amidst the chill, giggles ignite,
In the thread of twilight, pure delight.

The Cool Grasp of Twilight

Even the shadows start to sway,
As glacial breezes come out to play.
Snowflakes pirouette in the glow,
While frosty friends put on a show!

The squirrels sneak on ice capades,
While laughter trails in winter's shades.
With every chuckle, the cold feels bright,
In this cool grasp, we smile all night.

In the Arms of Stillness

In the morning light, we slip and slide,
A dance recited, so full of pride.
The snowmen laugh with carrot noses,
While squirrels plot their winter poses.

A penguin struts in a cozy hat,
Wondering where his ice cream's at.
Chasing snowflakes like they might bite,
Who knew that winter could be this bright?

A Sparkle of Iced Morning Light

Morning sprinkles, glittered delight,
A snowball fight breaks out, oh what a sight!
Laughter echoes through frosty trees,
As snowflakes tickle, like cheeky fleas.

Hot cocoa spills from laughing mugs,
While marshmallows float, like little bugs.
We'll build a fort, with walls so grand,
In this winter wonder, we make our stand.

The Unveiling of Winter's Palette

Colors swirl, with every gust,
The red-nosed reindeer out in the dust.
Painting cheeks with rosy cheer,
Jokes fly at the chill, nothing to fear.

Sleds race down the hills, oh so slick,
With snowmen dressed up, it's quite the trick!
Each twist and tumble, laughter peals,
Winter's humor is all it reveals.

Dancing Shadows on Crystal Shores

Footprints trace where the penguins roam,
Ice skates twirl, they've made this their home.
Shadows dance on the frozen lake,
While lovers share laughs and hot cakes.

The sun pops out, they throw a snowball,
Wiping the winter blues, one and all.
With every giggle, the day turns bright,
In this icy realm, we find our light.

The Breath of Crystal Mornings

Whispers of winter drift and sway,
Pajamas worn, I greet the day.
My nose is red, a glowing hue,
As cats prance round like they've got shoes.

Snowflakes dance on rooftops high,
While I fumble made of pie.
Coffee spills with a dainty splash,
I laugh as I slip, a comical crash.

When Ice Kisses the Ground

The ground is slick, a shiny show,
I waltz right in, my feet won't go.
Like a penguin on parade, I slip,
A windmill flaps, my legs do flip.

Trees adorned in coats of ice,
Little birds don't think twice.
They launch from branches, a cheerful squawk,
While I attempt my awkward walk.

The Quiet Elegance of Chill

In the hush of morning light,
I see my breath; it's quite a sight.
With scarves wrapped multiple times,
I sit and ponder silly rhymes.

Sipping tea, my fingers freeze,
Curled up tight, my knees at ease.
A sneeze erupts, with a frigid flair,
My cat jumps high—oh, what a scare!

A Tapestry of Frozen Dreams

Under twinkling stars so bright,
Dreams of snowmen fill the night.
They wear my old hat, a sight to see,
With carrots for noses, wild and free.

But wait, what's that? A scarf runs away!
On windy feet, it wants to play.
I chase it down the frosty lane,
In laughter's grip, I feel no pain.

Hues of White beneath the Moon

Snowflakes dance with tiny grace,
Painting ground in soft embrace.
A rabbit hops, then slips in play,
Wonders if he'll be on display!

Folks all bundled, hats askew,
Building snowmen, what a view!
Carrots for noses, buttons wide,
Laughing as they roll and slide.

The Silence that Embellishes the Snow

Whispers hush in snowy lanes,
Sleds scream down in merry trains.
A dog leaps out, his tail a blur,
Chasing snowflakes, a fluffy spur!

Plump snowballs 'gainst the fence,
Kids throw laughs without pretense.
The atom's quiet, see it thrive,
In giggles loud, we come alive!

Echoes of the Chill in the Night

Icicles hang with a cheeky glow,
Reminding us of things we know.
That slips and trips from clumsy feet,
Are part of winter's silly beat!

Under street lamps, shadows play,
As snowmen plot their great ballet.
A muffled 'oops' and then a cheer,
As they twirl 'round without a fear!

The Caress of Nature's Feather

Nature sprinkles joy with flair,
In every gust that twirls the air.
Hearts aglow, we chase our dreams,
In winter's chill, life brighter beams!

Each breath a cloud, we laugh and shout,
In frosty fun, there's no doubt.
From cozy homes, the world unique,
Winter's humor, warm and chic!

Glimmers on a Frozen Lake

Tiny ducks in woolly hats,
Sliding down on frozen mats.
A snowman with a carrot nose,
Tells the joke that nobody knows.

Pine trees wear their frosty bling,
Squirrels plot a winter fling.
They leap and twist, it's quite a sight,
Nutty love in the chilly night.

Icicles hang like silly teeth,
Chattering squirrels in disbelief.
They squeak and squawk, the jokes unroll,
Winter has claimed its comedic toll.

Watch a snowflake take a fall,
Land on noses, giggles call.
With rosy cheeks, we dance and prance,
In this icy wonderland romance.

The Haiku of a Winter's Breath

Chill breath whispers loud,
Snowsuit-clad kids tumble down,
What's that? A freeze tag!

Winter's breath is fun,
Hot cocoa warms up our hands,
Snowball fights a blast!

Chilled cheeks pink and bright,
Giggling as we run inside,
Mittens start a brawl.

A Gentle Chill Upon Awakening

Morning light meets icy air,
Coffee cups in hand we stare.
Outside the window, snowflakes play,
A chilly dance that's here to stay.

Cranky pants in puffy coats,
Sliding on snow, they boast and gloat.
But wait! Oh no, a tumble down,
Laughter rings from snow-clad town.

Snowball fights 'til faces red,
Snow-covered gnome peeks from his bed.
With clumsy grace, we take a spin,
Winter wins as we all grin.

The Stillness in the Air

In the quiet world so white,
A snowman takes a funny bite.
Birds on branches start to swap,
Pinecone hats, they never stop.

A chill creeps in, then giggles sprout,
Snowflakes play, there's no doubt.
With icy breath, we launch and flee,
As winter whispers, 'Come play with me!'

Ice skates glide with squeaky squeals,
As frosty air reveals our heels.
Laughter echoes through the trees,
In this winter's fresh, fun breeze!

Beneath a Silver Shroud

The trees wore coats of silver hue,
Each branch adorned with icy dew.
A squirrel sneezed, oh my, how loud!
He looked quite shocked beneath the shroud.

The ground was slick, a frozen slide,
I slipped and fell, my arms spread wide.
A penguin slid right past my nose,
And laughed aloud as I just froze.

Chilling Serenade of Dawn

The morning sun, a timid guest,
Peeks through clouds, a little stressed.
A crow complained of spiky chills,
While ice shoes danced on window sills.

The clock chimed loud, it's half past eight,
And here I am, still in debate.
To wear a coat or stay in bed?
The warmth of donuts fills my head.

Crystal Dreams on a Morning Chill

I thought I'd dream of summer sun,
But ice cubes crashed and spoilt the fun.
A snowman grinned with carrot glee,
And dared me forth for hot cocoa spree.

My mittens got stuck on my nose,
I chased my hat, but it arose.
The wind, a joker, played its game,
And tossed my scarf, oh what a shame!

Silken Breath of the Cold

The morning air, a silk embrace,
Made every breath a funny race.
A dog declared a battle cry,
And chased his tail—oh my, oh my!

As ponds reflected frozen grins,
Where penguins waltzed on icy fins.
I tried to join, but slipped and spun,
The dance of winter's just begun!

The Beauty of a Cold Embrace

The snowflakes dance like tiny fleas,
While squirrels wear scarves, oh what a tease!
Snowmen wobble with carrot noses,
As kids throw snowballs, their laughter poses.

The icicles hang like daggers from eaves,
While snowplows rumble, the entire town heaves.
Hot cocoa's calling, let's sip with glee,
Who knew winter would be such a spree?

With freezing fingers, we build a fort,
But then we stumble, falling short!
Giggles erupt, the cold's our friend,
In this icy chaos, let joy extend.

Veins of Silver Running Deep

The river's a popsicle, still as a mime,
As fish wear coats for a chilly swim time.
The ducks are waddling, but slipping around,
With flappy feet dancing on icy ground.

Snowflakes peek through the clouds with flair,
While meandering paths lead to nowhere, I swear!
The trees wear blankets, a sight so quirky,
Nature's dressed up in festive, fun murky.

Skating on ponds, a circus of sorts,
While grandmas giggle and heckle the sports.
Ice skates may wobble, but spirits won't drop,
In this wintry world, we leap, we hop!

The Stillness of Frozen Waters

The pond lies still, a shiny old plate,
Where frogs dream of croaking, but it's way too late.
The ice is a mirror, reflecting delight,
As skaters zoom past, what a comical sight!

With a gentle thud, the ice starts to crack,
The fish roll their eyes, "Oh, not this attack!"
Each slip and each slide adds giggles galore,
Who knew winter could be such a chore?

Icicles drip, a slow-motion show,
Turning into swords in a playful row.
While bunnies hop in their fluffy ball gowns,
Winter's a stage for laughter, not frowns.

Sighs of a Winter's Eve

On winter's eve, in blankets we snuggle,
While outside, the snowflakes begin their shuffle.
The cat gives a yawn, a master of pouts,
While dogs chase their tails, in thrilling bouts!

The streetlamps twinkle like stars on the ground,
And carolers sing, though slightly off sound.
Hot apple cider warms chilly bones,
Crackling fires pop with funny tones.

With every snowflake, a giggle we share,
In this chilly season, with laughter to spare.
For under the moonlight, we slip and we slide,
Let's dance with our hearts and let joy be our guide.

A Ballet of Ice and Light

In the morning, all is bright,
The trees wear coats, oh what a sight!
Squirrels slip and slide with glee,
In this frozen jubilee.

Little birds in wooly hats,
Huddle close with cheeky chats.
They dance atop the icy glaze,
And giggle through the chilly haze.

Snowmen strut with carrot noses,
Telling jokes about their poses!
But when the sun begins to peek,
They melt away, their laughter weak.

So raise a cup of cocoa high,
To all the friends who slip and fly!
In this frosty world of fun,
We laugh together, everyone!

Soft Echoes of Snowfall

Snowflakes tumble, soft and light,
Carefree dancers in their flight.
They tickle noses, kiss some cheeks,
While silly giggles spring from squeaks.

Pigeons puffed like fluffy clouds,
Strut around in frumpy crowds.
With each plop and playful fight,
They claim their thrones, all day and night.

Wooly mittens, mismatched too,
Untangle, twist—a playful brew!
Fingers cold, yet hearts feel warm,
In joys of winter's charming charm!

Dancers prance with snowball throws,
While laughter in the cold wind blows.
Together we embrace the chill,
With sparkling fun, a winter thrill!

Songs from the Heart of Winter

Legs all bundled, coats so bright,
Sliding down the hills, what a sight!
Laughter rings, a joyful sound,
As we tumble, roll around.

Chubby snowmen watching close,
With crooked smiles, as if to boast.
They tell tales of days gone by,
While snowflakes swirl and drift on high.

Hot cocoa poured in mugs so tight,
Marshmallows float like clouds in flight.
With each sip, a giggle grows,
As whipped cream lands right on our nose!

Winter nights by firelight's glow,
Echo laughter, soft and slow.
In this season, all feels bright,
Tunes of joy, each day and night!

The Hidden Secrets of Quiet Streams

Beneath the ice, the water flows,
Whispers secrets that nobody knows.
Fish with scarves swim to and fro,
Winking eyes, putting on a show.

Beavers dressed in tiny hats,
Sing their songs while chasing bats.
With branches floating, they build their dreams,
In this world of shimmering teams.

A frozen frog with a silly grin,
Practices croaks and a little spin.
While turtles laugh, cozy and round,
Sliding away without a sound.

Jack Frost must have a sense of fun,
With every joke, he's never done.
In winter's embrace, a playful state,
Nature giggles—it's never too late!

Radiance of the Pale Moon's Glow

The moon is like a silver coin,
Spilled out by a child's hand,
It giggles as it rolls away,
Bouncing off the frosty land.

Snowflakes dance with a cheeky grin,
Chasing squirrels up the trees,
They whisper secrets to the wind,
While making snowmen with ease.

The nights are cold; the stars do leer,
At folks who stumble with glee,
Building snow forts, sincere and proud,
Until they fall in, oh me!

Icicles hang like nature's teeth,
Laughing at the silly kids,
Who slip and slide, then shout in joy,
As winter's mischief quietly bids.

Traces of a Winter's Touch

A snowy blanket hides the ground,
With dogs in coats that match,
They dash around without a care,
While chasing after a snowball patch.

Snowmen wear hats that are too big,
One toppled over, such a sight!
His carrot nose fell off with style,
As children laughed with sheer delight.

A penguin waddles down the lane,
Thinking it's a frosty race,
But slips away with little grace,
As laughter echoes in this place.

With hot cocoa, we toast the chill,
While marshmallows float in the air,
A winter's prank on all of us,
Is wrapped in laughter everywhere.

Whispers of Winter's Embrace

The trees are dressed in crystals bright,
They twinkle like a disco ball,
While squirrels ask for a winter snack,
And dream of acorns—what a haul!

The wind starts blowing soft and low,
It tickles noses as we stroll,
While nearby laughter fills the air,
In frosty hats, we lose control.

Chasing snowflakes, we leap about,
As if we're caught in a silly game,
We trip and tumble, squeals abound,
Turning winter into a frame!

Each step we take brings muffled sounds,
Of giggles hidden under the snow,
With every slip, we shout aloud,
Who knew this chill could steal the show?

A Shimmering Silence

In the quiet of the snowy night,
The world looks dipped in milk,
But then a snowball comes from behind,
And suddenly it's chaos, not silk!

The silence breaks with joyful shrieks,
As laughter spills like melting ice,
A snowman shivers with surprise,
Now that's a winter sacrifice!

A hare jumps in a flurry of fun,
As children chase with sheer delight,
Their boots are soaked, their mittens lost,
But who cares? They'll dry by night!

With jolly hearts we run about,
Caught up in this frosty spree,
We find delight in every slip,
As winter giggles back at me!

A Dance of Frosted Petals

Snowflakes twirl with glee,
Like dancers wild and free.
They stumble, trip, and spin,
Creating laughter, bright and thin.

Every petal made of ice,
Jokes about their clumsy slice.
They whisper secrets, soft and quaint,
In playful giggles, they can't feign.

Nature giggles at the show,
As chilly breezes come and go.
They prance and leap, a chilly sight,
Chasing shadows in the light.

With each twinkling drop they fall,
They dance to nature's teasing call.
A winter's chuckle in the air,
Petals frosted, light as air.

The Spell of a Winter Night

The moon grins down with a wink,
Casting shadows that make you think.
Creatures chirp in muffled delight,
Singing songs of a frosty night.

Icicles dangle, sharp and sly,
Poking fun at the stars up high.
Whispers slice through the chilly breeze,
Tickling noses, oh what a tease!

The world wraps up in a fluffy cloak,
While giggling snowmen make a joke.
They nod and smile, all aglow,
As they watch the world twirl below.

Chill winds howl, but with a laugh,
Nature's trickster, on the path.
Under the spell, we can't resist,
Winter's jest, a frosty twist.

Echoes of the Whispering Chill

Whispers ride on the icy air,
Telling tales of frosty flair.
Chill giggles dart through the night,
Making shivers feel just right.

Trees shudder, branches sway,
In a funny, frosty ballet.
Each crunch beneath our busy feet,
Turns to laughter, oh so sweet!

The echoes bounce from hill to hill,
Silly sounds that give a thrill.
As snowmen wobble, doing their dance,
Nature's jesters take a chance.

With every swirl and quiet cheer,
The chilly chuckles draw us near.
In the winter's playful lore,
Joyful echoes forever soar.

A Canvas Woven in Ice

A canvas spread, pure and bright,
Crafted under the silver light.
Each frozen stroke, a giggling brush,
As winter paints without a rush.

Laughter bubbles in the streams,
Reflecting all our snowy dreams.
Scattered sparkles in a row,
Whispering secrets, soft and slow.

Snowmen line the frosted street,
Waving hands, with frosty feet.
They huddle close, in cozy glee,
Cracking jokes with the sprightly trees.

The world is wrapped in chilly cheer,
With a wink and nod from far and near.
As we dance on this glistening sea,
Joy rides high, so carefree.

The Velvet Grasp of Winter

The trees wear coats of fluffy white,
As squirrels skitter in delight,
They frolic and play, not a care in sight,
Nature's prankster, a chilly invite.

Snowmen stand with silly grins,
With carrot noses and twiggy chins,
They wave at passers with cheeky spins,
While laughter and giggles are where joy begins.

Icicles dangle, sharp as a knife,
But who knew they could bring such life?
They sparkle like crystals, causing some strife,
As kids take a tumble, landing with a whiff.

The air is crisp, the ground's a slide,
Winter's here with a playful stride,
Slip and slide, oh what a ride,
In the season where giggles and snowballs collide!

Frosted Breath of a Sleeping Earth

Under blankets of soft, glistening snow,
The world snoozes, wrapped up tight, you know,
A sleepy sigh from the ground below,
Dreams of spring in the chill's soft glow.

Rabbits bounce with coats all fluffed,
Chasing shadows, they're all quite stuffed,
In tunnels and burrows, cozy and cuffed,
Hiding from dawns that are chillily gruffed.

Down in the woods, the branches creak,
Winter's humor can be quite unique,
A whisper of jokes with every peak,
As the frozen streams gently squeak.

Nature chuckles, it's all in good fun,
With every snowflake, a laugh has begun,
In this world where the frost has spun,
It's a giggle-filled race, we all can run!

Gossamer Threads of Crystal Light

Morning breaks with a twinkle and shine,
The world adorned in a geometric line,
Every tree a diamond, a grand design,
With laughable shapes that are quite divine.

A spider spins from branch to branch,
Its web aglow in a winter's dance,
It seems to giggle, take every chance,
To catch a beam in a frosty romance.

Children's laughter echoes with glee,
As they build the tallest snow-sculpted tree,
Full of whimsy, as fun as can be,
In a world where the snowflakes agree.

So let's toast to the beauty so bright,
To all the wonders in the morning light,
With every sparkle, let joy take flight,
And laugh with the world, feeling just right!

A Gentle Kiss from the North

The wind whispers softly, a ticklish breeze,
Ruffling the hats, making laughter seize,
It nudges along with shivering tease,
While cheeks turn pink, as winter's freeze.

Hot cocoa spills in the playful mess,
As marshmallows bob, no need to stress,
With laughter that bubbles, a warm caress,
In every sip, winter's cozy dress.

Chasing snowflakes, flops and falls,
With every slip, the giggle calls,
Under the skies where bright snow sprawls,
In a kingdom of laughter, winter enthralls.

So cherish the moments, make merry and sound,
With snowball fights that know no bound,
In the cuddle of winter, joy can be found,
In a world where fun and frost are crowned!

Frosty Murmurs of an Ancient Tale

In the chill of a winter's fair,
Squirrels wear scarves with flair,
They chatter in tiny, squeaky tones,
Trading secrets with icy stones.

A snowman's grin, somewhat absurd,
Complains that he's never heard,
Of a carrot's pointy ploy,
To steal the heart of every toy.

Snowflakes dance like giggling sprites,
Tickling noses in frosty bites,
They tumble and twist, the whimsical crew,
As if teaching winter a playful view.

Old trees don hats made of white,
Wondering how they lost the fight,
Against the winds that twist and tease,
And wear their branches like a sneeze.

A Serenade in Icy Whispers

In the glimmer of a chilly night,
Penguins practice their snowball fight,
With flippers raised and laughter loud,
They form a very wobbly crowd.

Icicles dangle, sharp as a knife,
Dish out advice on winter strife,
"Watch your step, or slip you might,"
They giggle in the pale moonlight.

The stars above, all twinkling bright,
Join in the fun, a wondrous sight,
Winking at the snowmen below,
Claiming they're stars for their show.

A snowball flies with cheeky grace,
Landing right on a gnome's face,
Who blushes red, though made of stone,
Grinning wide, he's never alone.

The Lure of Subdued Light

A lantern's glow in the snowy park,
Attracts a raccoon, quite the lark,
With goggles on, he's on a quest,
To find the snacks he loves the best.

The shadows play a game of tag,
While hippos in sweaters always brag,
About their winter fashion sense,
As they slide past with a mischief tense.

A crisp breeze whispers silly tales,
Of drifts and whirls and chilled gales,
While trees debate on their new names,
Like 'Fabulous' and 'Ony-Fame'.

The moon winks down, a subtle tease,
Echoing laughter in the freeze,
As everyone perks up with delight,
In this frosty, fun, magical night.

Notes from a Crystal Serenade

In a frosty woods where the berries gleam,
A rabbit hums an old winter theme,
With snow-globes swirling, round he prances,
Mimicking reindeer and silly dances.

Dancing lights begin to sway,
Sending shivers in a playful way,
As snowflakes giggle, flitting by,
Winking bright from the azure sky.

A snow-dog barks at a shadowed trout,
Playing fetch, with a loud shout,
The river skims, all fluffed up tight,
Baffled by the winter's light bite.

The air is filled with merry sounds,
As laughter echoes through the grounds,
Creating joy with every chill,
A happy tune through winter's thrill.

Secrets Beneath the Snow

Beneath the white, where secrets hide,
A squirrel lost its winter pride.
Searching for snacks, he digs in vain,
Finding only a chilled champagne.

A rabbit hops, with quite a flair,
In fuzzy boots, he shuffles there.
He slips and slides, what a display!
As icy snow makes him ballet.

A fox sneezes, oh what a sound!
He blames the snowflakes all around.
With nose so cold, he gives a huff,
Yet still he prances, that's enough!

The trees wear coats of shimmering sheen,
And join the dance, a whimsical scene.
With branches swaying, they all prance,
In nature's ball, they twirl and dance.

Nature's Cool Caress

The chill of dawn, a playful tease,
Icicles hang like frozen keys.
A penguin waddles with such speed,
His splashes fly—it's quite a deed!

A snowman grins with buttons bright,
His carrot nose, a funny sight.
He jokes with birds that dare to land,
"Don't eat my hat, I'm not that bland!"

The clouds above begin to drip,
As children cheer and take a trip.
They catch the flakes, a flurry's fun,
While snowballs fly, they start to run!

As evening falls, the stars give glee,
A blanket of white, oh so carefree.
With laughter echoing through the night,
Nature's chill brings pure delight!

Celestial Touches of Winter

A moonbeams zip through branches bare,
Painting the world with frosty flair.
The squirrels toast with acorn cups,
While penguins take their funny jumps!

The owl, with wisdom, starts to hoot,
He tells the tales of winter's loot.
With laughs and chuckles in the air,
The night unfolds—a silly affair!

The stars above begin to twinkle,
While snowflakes dance and playfully sprinkle.
With every flake that lands in grace,
A giggle erupts from the chilly space.

In this cool world, where giggles flow,
The night shines bright, all aglow.
And laughter echoes through the trees,
In winter's grasp, the heart's at ease.

Embracing the Stillness

In silent woods where laughter beams,
The snow banks cradle all our dreams.
A rabbit dons a scarf too bold,
While deer watch on, amused, yet cold.

A snowball fight breaks the still air,
With cheers and squeals, no time to spare.
The shovels clash, oh what a scene,
In nature's fun, they play the queen!

With frozen cheeks and noses bright,
They twirl and tumble, pure delight.
The chilly breeze, it tickles too,
As laughter echoes, it feels so new.

In winter's arms, we find our play,
Through every flake, in childlike sway.
A joyful romp, a playful trance,
Embracing stillness, join the dance!

Elegy for a Frosty Dawn

The dawn arrived with a sneeze,
A chill that brought a tease.
The sun just snickered from afar,
While I stumbled, my nose ajar.

The icy air, a prankster's delight,
I shivered and chuckled at the sight.
My coffee mug, a frozen block,
Who knew it would become a rock?

The trees donned coats of white fluff,
Thought they could dance, but it was tough.
With every step, I slipped and spun,
Laughter echoed, winter's pun.

Yet amidst this frozen ballet,
We turn our hearts to play the day.
For in the chill, we find our smile,
As the frost nudges us all the while.

Chilling Tranquility of the Night Sky

The stars twinkled with a wink,
As I fumbled with my drink.
A blanket of ice all around,
I laughed at how I nearly drowned.

The moon chuckled, a gleeful grin,
While I slipped on ice—who would win?
A squirrel skidded, a fuzzy flight,
In winter's glow, what a sight!

The night was quiet, but oh so sly,
As I watched an owl roll by.
With every hoot, a fresh surprise,
As the cold night made us wise.

So here I sit with roasted toes,
In this world where hilarity grows.
With a shiver and a grin so wide,
In chilly peace, we take our ride.

The Timeless Dance of Winter's Veil

The snowflakes jived in the air,
While I tried to tango with a chair.
Each step on ice a comic scene,
I laughed till my sides turned green.

The trees were twirling in their coats,
While penguins practiced their vote.
"Who can slide the farthest, let's see!"
A challenge born of sheer glee.

With cheeks that looked like rosy fruits,
I joined the dance in thick winter boots.
A swirl, a twirl, a noble slip,
As nature laughed, we took our trip.

So here's to winter's silly grace,
With frostbitten toes in this funny place.
In timeless dance beneath the stars,
We find the joy, no matter how far.

Emotions Wrapped in Snowy Quiet

In the quiet, emotions play,
Snowflakes whisper, "Let's be gay!"
A pause, a puff, a chilly breath,
In this moment, we conquer death.

With laughter wrapped in frozen wraps,
I tripped on snow, oh, those mishaps!
The world around, a silent cheer,
Each tumble echoed, "Have no fear!"

Snowmen chuckled with carrot grins,
While I debated where joy begins.
The stillness held a funny tune,
As I danced beneath the moon.

So here we pause, in snowy delight,
With giggles echoing through the night.
For in this hush, we find our muse,
Wrapped in mirth, we cannot lose.

Whispers of the Chilled Dawn

Chill in the air, I shiver and shake,
Nibbling on pancakes, that's my mistake!
A squirrel in a scarf, looking quite dapper,
While I stumble on ice, like a clumsy flapper.

Hot cocoa spills as I dance with a broom,
The cat gives me looks, as if I'll bring doom.
Snowflakes descend with mischief and glee,
Tickling my nose, oh, can't you just see?

Caress of Winter's Veil

The trees wear white hats, so quirky and spry,
A penguin on roller skates zooms right by.
I slip on a patch, oh what a misstep,
My laughter echoes, as I lose my prep.

Snowmen hold parties, they dance in a row,
With twigs for their arms, they put on a show.
A carrot for a nose, what a sight to behold,
They chuckle at me, as my handle I fold.

The Tender Touch of Ice

Icicles hang like daggers of play,
While I trip on the ice in an elegant sway.
A dog in a sweater, he sings 'Let it Snow!'
As I shoo off the frost that won't let me go.

The hedgehog's bundled, all snug as a bug,
He wiggles and giggles, gives me a shrug.
With each frosty breath, I'm laughing anew,
This chilly frolic just never feels blue.

Embrace of the Quiet White

The world's cloaked in glee, with snowflakes galore,
But here comes my neighbor, with his wild, loud snore.
He's building a fort, a kingdom of freeze,
While I play infantry, slipping with ease.

Laughter erupts, as we both make a splash,
Rolling in snow, oh look at us crash!
In this wintry land, fun never gets cold,
With giggles and grins, joy will unfold.

The Subtle Art of Winter's Breath

A whisper of chill in the air,
I slip on ice like a thoroughfare.
Socks now my rival, slippery foes,
You'd think I'd learned, but winter still throws.

Snowflakes dance like they've lost their minds,
They tumble and twirl, leaving no signs.
On every small hill, a sled waits to be,
But somehow, it just ends up with me!

Hot cocoa requires marshmallows, you see,
Yet they melt like dreams under winter's spree.
I take a sip, but my tongue's on fire,
What was supposed to warm me, backfires dire!

So here's to the season with giggles and glee,
Where laughter is loud, wild, and free.
For under the sun, the snow may be grand,
But inside my home, I'm stuck like the sand.

Shadows of the Frosted Moon

The moon glows bright, a gleam on white,
Casting shadows that leap with delight.
Elves in my yard, or so I believe,
Or maybe just squirrels that dare to deceive!

Icicles hang like chandeliers crusted,
I reach for one, my fingers are rusted.
Snap! Off it goes, my hand now in shock,
But the laughter rings out with a hearty knock!

Snowmen stand tall, with carrots askew,
A fashion faux pas, what could they do?
Top hats and scarves, they're dapper for sure,
Yet no one can say how to make them endure.

Midnight arrives, with giggles and cheers,
I trip on a snowdrift, let out a sneer.
Yet in all of this silliness, I see,
Winter's charm is a dance made for me!

The Glistening Realm of Winter

In a world of glimmer, it's all here to see,
Snow drifts glitter like bad jewelry.
I slip down a path with a laugh and a fall,
The ice plays tricks, oh, winter's a ball!

Candles flicker, and embers ignite,
Hot soup spills over, what a funny sight!
The cat chases shadows, does backflips in glee,
While I try to balance, just an old clumsy me!

Bundled up tight, I venture outside,
My nose turns pink, like it's taken a ride.
But the hot air balloon of my cheeks feels so great,
Winter's comedian – it keeps me in fate!

Tiny snowflakes fall, like confetti galore,
As I sneak in the door, with my friends who adore.
Together we chuckle at every little blunder,
For even the weather can't silence our thunder!

When Time Pauses in Snow

Snow blankets the world, a calming retreat,
But inside the house, chaos stirs with a beat.
Kids throw themselves, it's a flurry of fun,
While I sip my tea, my worries weigh a ton!

Time hangs still; it's a magical ruse,
Outside the blizzard claims it's got the blues.
Sleds zip and zoom, what a clatter they make,
As I scream, "Watch out!" for goodness' sake!

Under the stars, all glistening bright,
I trip on the step, oh, what a sight!
Laughter erupts as I tumble and roll,
Winter's got jokes — it's a comic's whole goal!

So here's to the blunders, the slips, and the slides,
To mugs filled with laughter where giggling resides.
In this frozen wonderland, joy's not a chore,
Let's embrace the madness, each flake we adore!

The Stillness of the Icy Whisper

The trees are dressed in sparkling lace,
They giggle softly, a chilly embrace.
Squirrels shiver in their fuzzy coats,
While snowflakes dance like little boats.

A rabbit hops, but slips on the ground,
He does a twist, then turns around.
The world is quiet, except for the crack,
A lowly sound of a snowman's snack.

The sun peeks out with a cheeky grin,
As winter's jokes begin to spin.
The air is fresh, like minty breath,
Each frostbite giggle teeters near death.

Icicles hang like dangly charms,
While snowmen feign their icy arms.
A snowball fight, oh what a scene,
Nature's jesters, all in between.

Frosted Morning's Lullaby

The dawn breaks softly, a chilly cheer,
While yawned-out grannies sip warm beer.
Under covers, they sneak a look,
At the cold that's crept like a funny book.

Penguins slide on their little belly,
Squeaking out tunes, oh how they jelly!
Children shout with laughter's bell,
As snowflakes dance, casting their spell.

The rooftops wear their frosty crown,
As winter holds its belly down.
A dog skids past, tail like a flag,
And in his wake, a frozen drag!

Each breath a cloud, white puffs afloat,
Like cotton candy, what a remote!
Winter's charm, with giggles abound,
Through frosted mornings, joy is found.

Nature's Soft Embrace in White

In blankets thick, the world is wrapped,
Where every tree seems gently tapped.
Birds fluff up as if to boast,
While snow drifts down, like a winter toast.

A clumsy deer, with a slip and slide,
Makes a graceful mess, though it tried to hide.
Snowdrops chuckle as they pop up bright,
In the midst of a giggling winter night.

The sun peeks through a frosted veil,
As creatures play without fail.
A hedgehog snuffles, looking for snacks,
While a squirrel laughs, dodging its tracks.

Each moment's wrapped in chilly jest,
It's nature's way to keep us blessed.
So let us dance, let spirits soar,
In soft embrace, forevermore.

The Glimmering Fragrance of Winter

Amidst the chill, there's a scent so sweet,
Like cookies baking, a winter treat.
Noses twitch in the frosty air,
As laughter echoes from everywhere.

Snowmen boast their carrot noses,
While frosty friends strike funny poses.
A cat walks soft, tail held high,
Wondering why the squirrels fly by.

Snowball hands in a carefree flurry,
Everything sparkles; oh, what a hurry!
With each skid and slip, joy spreads wide,
In the magical world where giggles abide.

A winter's yarn, spun full of cheer,
Jokes hidden among the white veneer.
So twirl and spin, let laughter ignite,
Winter's fragrance keeps spirits bright.

Echoes of a Frigid Dawn

Chill nibbles at the cheek, oh dear,
A snowman grins with frosty cheer.
His carrot nose, a wobbly sight,
He sneezes snowflakes at first light.

The sun peeks up, the snowflakes dance,
A penguin slips, oh what a chance!
With flailing wings, it makes a scene,
A winter laugh, so sweet and keen.

Icicles hang like nature's bling,
They drip and drop, a sweaty thing.
The groundhog pops his furry head,
Says, "Please no more of winter's dread!"

With giggles ringing in the air,
Hot cocoa waits, with marshmallows rare.
For winter's tricks, we raise a toast,
A chilly dance, we love the most!

Fragile Petals in a Winter's Grasp

Petals wrapped in chilly white,
They shiver, shudder, what a fright!
A daffodil in snow's embrace,
With floral frown, it masks its face.

The tulips poke from icy ground,
Giving winter a cheeky sound.
"Where's the sun?" they squawk and plead,
In this frozen world, they surely heed.

Squirrels in scarves, a jolly sight,
Dancing round in winter's spite.
With acorns clipped, they do the jig,
While snowflakes twirl, oh what a gig!

Yet when spring bursts through the door,
Those petals grin, oh, what's in store?
They wink at winter, "Not so fast!"
A flowery punchline, winter's cast!

The Soft Lullaby of Ice

In the quiet, the ice sings low,
A melody of twinkling snow.
Snowflakes giggle as they fall,
In winter's arms, we hear them call.

The critters wrapped in cozy wear,
A raccoon snoozes without a care.
His dreams of nuts, a merry feast,
In frosty realms, he's quite the beast.

Jack Frost plays a cheeky tune,
With silver bells beneath the moon.
The trees all waltz in chilly air,
While snowmen break into a flare.

As evening hush brings twinkling stars,
We gather 'round with giggles and jars.
Hot drinks in hand, we toast the chill,
In laughter's warmth, we find the thrill!

Beneath the Veil of White

Beneath a blanket soft and white,
The world looks cute, a pure delight.
A pup pounces in the freezing air,
With flurries flying everywhere.

Old snowmen with a crooked grin,
Stand guard while snowballs fly within.
The kids all cheer, their laughter bright,
As winter plays with all its might.

A hedgehog peeks—don't be a fool,
Cuddle up, it's winter's rule.
With icy breath and frosty toes,
He hibernates; that's how it goes.

In jolly rounds, we gather near,
For tales of whimsy filled with cheer.
So underneath this wintry cloak,
A toast to fun with every joke!

Glow of the Winter Stars

In the night, the stars twinkle bright,
Like diamonds tossed in a playful fight.
Snowmen dance with their carrot noses,
While rabbits hop 'round like winter posies.

Icicles hang like shiny spears,
As squirrels gather round, facing their fears.
A snowball flies, misses its mark,
Land on the dog, who then makes a spark!

A snowflake lands on my warm cup,
Cocoa's in danger, oh what a hiccup!
With each giggle, the chill starts to fade,
We laugh so hard, the cold's mislaid.

Winter's a jester, with tricks up its sleeve,
Playing pranks, never wanting to leave.
So let's cheer, for the night's just begun,
With mischief and joy, we're all having fun!

The Poetry of Hushed Landscapes

In the stillness, whispers softly play,
Puffy clouds drift like children at play.
Hushed landscapes wear a picturesque gown,
While silly snowflakes swirl all around.

Frozen ponds like mirrors of cheer,
Skaters giggle, not showing fear.
While one takes a tumble, cheeks full of snow,
Laughter erupts, setting fears aglow.

Trees wear blankets of white so divine,
Their branches droop, forming a line.
A squirrel giggles, slips on a branch,
Tripping right into a frosty dance!

The sun peeks out, sharing a grin,
Joining our wintery fun with a spin.
Every moment a charming delight,
Hushed landscapes giggle through the night!

Crystalline Threads of Serenity

Wisps of frost dance on the edge,
Like tiny fairies made of an ice wedge.
There's humor in every crystal thread,
As gnomes slip past with a nod and a spread.

The trees wear coats of glimmering lace,
Watching the antics in a slow-motion race.
With each twirl of a snowball thrown,
The table's set for winter's own throne!

Flakes flutter down in a flurry of glee,
While children shout, "Catch me if you see!"
And giggling elders rush with surprise,
Joining in chaos, all joy in their eyes.

Serenity sparkles like glittering cheer,
In the quiet, there's laughter, resounding clear.
So embrace silly joys, as they twine and weave,
For winter's a stage, let's play and believe!

The Twilight of Chilling Breezes

Twilight settles with a chilly shiver,
As branches sway, cold winds deliver.
Snowflakes twirl, causing a flurry,
While kites of skaters dash in a hurry.

With mittens flapping like birds on a breeze,
We dodge the snowballs, aiming our knees.
Old folks chuckle, recalling their youth,
Sledding down hills and sharing the truth.

While laughter rings out, they slip and slide,
Yet camaraderie warms this wintery ride.
The dogs join in, barking with glee,
As they tumble and roll, so wild and free.

The night draws near, with twinkling lights,
Hustle and bustle, what winter ignites.
In the twilight, let silliness spread,
For laughter and warmth live well in our head!

Laces of Light upon the Earth

The shimmering glow, a giggle so bright,
Sprinkles of laughter that dance in the night.
A tap on the cheek, like a playful tease,
Nature's pulse quickens with whimsical ease.

Snowflakes tumble like clumsy ballet,
Waltzing on rooftops, they lock in a fray.
The ground wears a blanket, so soft and so white,
While critters in mittens romp through delight.

Squirrels in hats and rabbits in boots,
Strut through the garden like fancy old brutes.
Each step brings a chuckle, a slip or a slide,
In this woeful frolic, there's nowhere to hide.

Laces of light weave a story so grand,
In the frosty theatre where mischief is planned.
With giggles and glimmers, all hearts set aglow,
This frosted affair is a laugh-filled show.

A Chill that Whispers

A chill that chuckles, it flirts with the trees,
Tickling the branches, they bend with such ease.
Whispers of glee in the shivering air,
Poking at noses, with nibbles to spare.

The moon grins down like a cheeky old chap,
Winking at shadows that squirm in a nap.
With branches all creaking like old wooden doors,
The night has a sense of the silliest scores.

Cold marbles of ice, they giggle and pry,
Hiding 'neath leaves, oh my, how they lie!
They trick all the puddles, inviting a splash,
With every clean tumble, the laughter's a bash.

So let's raise a toast, to the frost and the fun,
To the nippy old shivers, our party's begun.
With every snowflake that flutters and falls,
We weave through the magic, our joy softly calls.

The Frosted Canvas of Nature

On a canvas of whimsy, the world comes alive,
With doodles and frolics where chuckles derive.
Brush strokes of laughter, so brilliant and bright,
Paint nature's attire in pure moonlit light.

The pines wear their crowns made of glistening pearl,
While buzzing bees tease as they twirl and they whirl.
A canvas, oh splendid, with patterns that prance,
Underneath the soft canvas, the creatures all dance.

With chubby-cheeked snowmen, all grinning so wide,
And penguins on ice, they just giggle and slide.
Every flake is a spark of a laugh in the air,
Creating a masterpiece, so silly, so rare.

So let's tiptoe softly through this frosted dream,
Where laughter is sprinkled like whipped-up cream.
With a jocular brushstroke, the world's painted bright,
Each moment's a treasure, a chuckle in flight.

Veils of Icicles and Dreams

Veils of icicles dangle and sway,
Like party streamers on a chilly buffet.
They twinkle and jingle like tiny small bells,
In this frosty kingdom where laughter dwells.

The rooftops are frosted with sugary flakes,
While snowmen have parties and bake silly cakes.
Their noses made of carrots, grinning with glee,
As they plan all the mischief that's crafty and free.

The windows are frosted with laughter so light,
As shadows play games, weaving joy in the night.
Each breath brings a giggle, a puff in the air,
As icicles sway like they're dancing without care.

So join in the frolic, let whimsy take flight,
With veils of old glee to guide us tonight.
For the chill that surrounds us is filled with surprise,
In the playful embrace of our wintry skies.

Harmony in the Whisper of Ice

In the quiet chill, a giggle plays,
Ice jokes cracking in frosty rays.
Snowmen waltzing in a wobbly dance,
With carrot noses, they seize their chance.

The world's a stage in winter's guise,
Sleds fly by with gleeful cries.
Hot cocoa smiles warm the day,
While snowflakes drop in a fluffy display.

A Moment Caught in Time's Embrace

Time stands still, with a playful wink,
As icy whispers make us think.
A snowball fight begins with glee,
With laughter ringing, wild and free.

Penguins shuffling in socks of white,
As we slip and slide in pure delight.
Each chilly breath, a puff in the air,
Creating laughter everywhere.

Lullaby of Sparkling Snowflakes

Twinkling kisses from heavens above,
Ice-dusted dreams, winter's soft love.
Snowflakes giggle, landing near,
Playing tag as they swirl and cheer.

Piles of fluff, a throne for the brave,
Upon snowy hills, we joyously crave.
Frosty whispers wrapped in cheer,
Tickling noses, bringing us near.

Tracing Patterns on a Frozen Canvas

Footprints dance on a canvas bright,
Sketches of joy in the pale moonlight.
Snowballs roll, forming laughter anew,
With each chilly toss, we paint the view.

A snowflake's giggle, a shimmering tease,
Each falls softly, like a chill breeze.
Artful shapes in a wintry spree,
Nature's canvas calls out to thee.

Ethereal Tapestry of Chill

In the morning light he plays,
Dancing on the rooftops' haze.
Icicles hang like hefty gents,
Making roofs lose their contents.

The lawn transformed, looks quite bizarre,
Like confetti near the car.
Snowmen wobble, wave hello,
Awaiting sun's warm, sunny show.

Whiskers glisten, cats take flight,
Chasing snowflakes in delight.
The chilly air spills laughter sweet,
As penguins trot on tiny feet.

With coffee mugs, cold hands we warm,
As snowflakes swirl in crazy form.
The world turned white, it seems so grand,
While squirrels plot their grain-filled plans.

Enchantment of the Winter's Grasp

A wintry spell grips all around,
Neighbors in snowball fights abound.
Tumbling down from frosty heights,
The giggles soar like kites in flight.

Socks on hands, the new trend's in,
Winter's fashion—may we win?
We dress like marshmallows on parade,
In this frosty escapade.

The dog's a snowball, round and wild,
Chasing flakes like a joyful child.
He rolls and spins, a furry blur,
While winter warms his furry fur.

Hot cocoa spills in boisterous cheer,
As laughter echoes, crystal clear.
The magic in each icy breath,
Bares the joy of winter's wealth.

Subtle Artistry of the Frosted Air

Delicate swirls on windowpanes,
Nature's art in chilly chains.
The cat, he ponders with a glare,
Watching coldness paint the air.

Snowflakes giggle, tickle noses,
While winter's charm in coldness dozes.
A snow fort rises, epic goal,
'Tis the season of snowball patrol.

Gloves mismatched, a fashion blunder,
As children laugh and skies grow thunder.
The paths are slick, we slip and slide,
Oh what a ride on winter's tide!

Pine trees wear their snowy hats,
Squirrels tease while chatting bats.
Amidst the cold, warmth starts to spark,
In joy we find our favorite park!

Serene Silhouette of Icebound Trees

Under trees, their branches bowed,
Icicle chandeliers, oh so proud!
The branches drip with nature's bling,
While snowflakes drop and winter sings.

A frosty breeze whispers jokes and cheer,
While icy wonders slowly appear.
The world dressed up for winter's play,
As snowflakes tumble in their ballet.

Meanwhile, my nose, it grows so red,
Hot soup awaits, but I'd rather dread.
With every slip, I squeal and grin,
A dance of folly in the spin!

As icicles dangle, an artist's dream,
Nature crafts a joyful theme.
In winter's hush, we find such bliss,
With frosty laughter, we play like this.